Written by Pamela Hickman • Illustrated by Heather Collins

THE KIDS CANADIAN

Tree

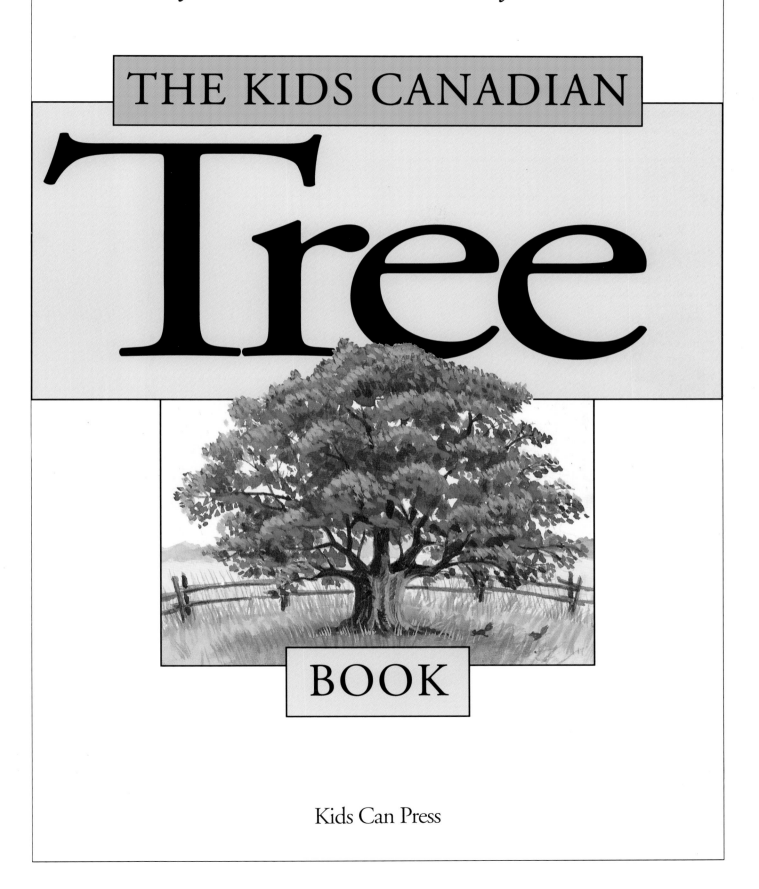

BOOK

Kids Can Press

First U.S. edition 1999

Text © 1995 Pamela Hickman
Illustrations © 1995 Heather Collins/Glyphics

Kids Can Press acknowledges the financial support of the Government of Canada, through the BPIDP, for our publishing activity.

Published in Canada by
Kids Can Press Ltd.
29 Birch Avenue
Toronto, ON M4V 1E2

www.kidscanpress.com

Edited by Trudee Romanek
Series editor: Laurie Wark
Designed by Blair Kerrigan/Glyphics

Printed in Hong Kong by Wing King Tong Company Limited

The hardcover edition of this book is smyth sewn casebound.
The paperback edition of this book is limp sewn with a drawn-on cover.

CDN 95 0 9 8 7 6 5 4 3 2 1
CDN PA 95 0 9 8 7 6 5 4 3 2

Canadian Cataloguing in Publication Data

Hickman, Pamela
  The kids Canadian tree book

(Kids Canadian nature series)
Includes index.

ISBN 1-55074-198-5 (bound) ISBN 1-55074-336-8 (pbk.)

1. Trees — Canada — Juvenile literature. I. Collins, Heather. II. Title. III. Series: Hickman, Pamela. Kids Canadian nature series.

QK201.H53 1995   j582.160971   C95-930640-4

Kids Can Press is a Nelvana company

Acknowledgements

Many thanks to my editors, Laurie Wark and Trudee Romanek, to Lori Burwash for coordinating so many schedules, and to our book designer, Blair Kerrigan. Thanks also to my family for their enthusiasm throughout our adventures in making maple syrup.

For James,
Catherine and
Rebecca Hunter
PH

CONTENTS

Meet a tree

Do you like to climb trees, sit under their shady branches on a hot summer's day, eat apples and peaches, read books or watch birds? If you said yes to any of these, then trees are already an important part of your life. Canada is one of the most forested countries in the world. Trees provide food and shelter for wildlife, they help to keep the soil, water and air healthy, and their wood is used for lumber and paper. Whether you live in a forest in British Columbia, a city in Ontario or on the prairie grassland, you depend on trees every day. Canada has over 140 native tree species. Many kinds of trees from other parts of the world are planted in gardens and parks, too.

Take a look at the trees on these pages and discover how different kinds of trees from coast to coast have lots in common.

a trunk of wood protected by a covering of bark

roots to suck up water and minerals from the soil

leaves to make
food for the tree

all trees
produce
seeds

branches

Two kinds of trees

Have you ever noticed that some trees lose all their leaves in the fall, but other trees stay green all year around? There are two kinds of trees: deciduous and coniferous. Trees that lose their broad leaves in the fall and grow a new set in the spring are called deciduous. Oaks and birches are deciduous trees. Coniferous trees, or conifers, such as pine and spruce, shed their old leaves, or needles, too. But they lose only a few at a time and new needles grow in before all the old ones fall off.

In the spring, deciduous trees have flowers. When the flowers are pollinated they produce seeds, which are often inside a fruit such as an apple or a beech nut. Conifers have cones instead of flowers. They produce seeds, but no fruit.

White Pine

White Oak

Two in one

Larch trees are two kinds of trees at once. They are coniferous because they have cones instead of flowers. But they are also deciduous, since they lose all of their needles in the fall and grow new ones the next spring.

OPEN AND CLOSE SESAME

After a forest fire, Jack Pines are the first trees to start growing. That's because their cones are opened by the heat of the fire and the seeds are released. After the fire, Jack Pine seeds are ready to grow on the newly burned ground, without competing with other plants for space.

White Pine cones have light dry seeds so that the wind can blow them to new places to grow. Their cones close up when it rains to keep the seeds dry. The cones open again on sunny days so the ripe seeds can be blown away. You can watch cones in action with this simple experiment.

You'll need:

2 Jack Pine or Scotch Pine cones

a cookie sheet

an oven

2 dry White Pine or hemlock cones with open scales

a large bowl of water

paper towel

Jack Pine

Scotch Pine

hemlock

White Pine

1. Put one Jack Pine or Scotch Pine cone on the cookie sheet and ask an adult to put it in the oven at 150°C (300°F) for 15 minutes. Leave the other cone on the counter.

2. Compare the heated cone to the one on the counter.

3. Place a White Pine or hemlock cone in the bowl of water for 15 minutes. Leave the other cone on the counter for comparison.

4. Compare the wet and dry cones. Place the wet cone on a paper towel and let it dry. What happens to the cone as it dries?

Leaves up close

Look at the trees in your neighbourhood. What colour are their leaves? Most trees have green leaves because they are filled with a chemical called chlorophyll (say clor-o-fil). Chlorophyll helps the leaves make food to keep the trees healthy and to help them grow. The chlorophyll in the leaves uses energy from the sun, water from the soil and carbon dioxide from the air to make sugars, or glucose, to feed the trees. This process is called photosynthesis.

Leaves come in all different shapes and sizes. Some leaves are whole, or undivided, like a maple leaf, and they are called simple leaves. Others, such as sumac leaves, are divided into tiny parts called leaflets. A sumac leaf is a kind of compound leaf.

Check out the leaves in your yard or local park. Can you find some simple leaves and some compound leaves? Look for leaves that have smooth edges and others that have little teeth along their edges. Leaves are important clues to helping you identify trees.

White Birch

Weeping Willow

Sugar Maple

hickory

Linden

sumac

ash

Red Oak

8

Make a leaf collection

You can gather green leaves in the summer and colourful leaves in the fall to make a collection. Collect as many different kinds of leaves as you can find on the ground. Glue or tape your leaves onto sheets of three-ringed paper. Beside each leaf, write where you found it, the date and what kind of tree it came from, if you know. Cover each sheet with clear plastic wrap and store the sheets in a binder.

You can make your leaves last longer by waxing them before you attach them to the paper. To wax leaves, place them between two sheets of waxed paper. Lay a cloth over the top sheet and ask an adult to press your leaves with a hot iron. The heat from the iron will melt the wax onto the leaves. The wax coating will keep your leaves from drying out or fading.

Why do leaves change colour?

When the summertime greens of deciduous leaves turn to the reds, yellows, oranges and purples of fall, you know that winter is coming. Have you ever wondered where the bright autumn colours come from? The yellows and oranges are actually in the leaves all summer long, but they are hidden by the stronger green colour of chlorophyll. When fall comes, leaves stop making chlorophyll. Soon afterward the green colour disappears and the other colours take over.

HIDDEN COLOURS

You can find the hidden colours in green leaves with this simple activity.

You'll need:

some green leaves

a wide-mouth jar

rubbing alcohol

a spoon

scissors

a coffee filter

tape

a pencil

1. Tear the leaves into little bits and put them in the jar with enough rubbing alcohol to cover them.
Caution: rubbing alcohol is poisonous. Ask an adult for help when using it.

2. Stir the mixture and then leave it for about five minutes. Colours from the leaves will dissolve in the rubbing alcohol.

3. Cut a strip 4 cm wide and 9 cm long from your coffee filter. Tape one end to the middle of your pencil.

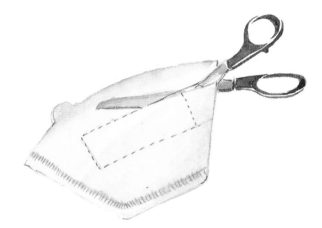

4. Rest the pencil across the mouth of the jar so that the bottom of the filter strip hangs into the rubbing-alcohol solution.

5. Watch as the filter strip soaks up the solution. When the filter paper is wet nearly to the top, lift it out of the jar and lay it on some paper to dry.

6. When the filter paper is dry, you will see different bands of colour, which represent the colours in the leaves. Look for green, orange and yellow.

7. Try this activity with colourful fall leaves. Do you see a green band on your filter paper?

Trees in winter

Some animals sleep through winter to save energy and to avoid the freezing cold. Trees also go into a kind of resting period in the winter and stop growing. In the warm weather, the leaves of deciduous trees use a lot of water to make food for the tree. As long as there is enough water in the soil, the tree stays healthy. But in the winter when the ground is frozen, the tree can't get any water. To survive, the tree must save as much water as possible. To stop water from being lost through the leaves, a thin layer, like a scab, grows between the tree branch and the leaf, cutting the leaf off from the tree's supply of water and minerals. Eventually each leaf falls off the tree.

scab

Take a look at a deciduous tree in winter. Its bare branches and grayish brown or white bark almost make the tree look dead. If you take a close-up look at the branches and twigs, though, you will see tiny buds at their tips and along their sides. These buds are like little packages, packed full of next spring's beautiful leaves and flowers. Check out the twigs of different trees and you'll find that buds come in all sorts of shapes, sizes and textures. Many buds are sticky with a waterproof resin that keeps the leaves inside warm and dry.

A big, old oak tree may drop 700 000 leaves in the fall. How long would it take you to rake all of them up?

Peek into a bud

In late winter or early spring, find a few different buds, the larger the better. Peel away the outer bud scales with your fingers or some tweezers. Inside the bud you will find the tiny, folded-up beginnings of the new leaves of spring. When the ground thaws in spring and the tree roots can suck up lots of water again, the buds begin to swell and grow as they take on water. Eventually the buds burst out of their coverings, and the tiny, pale, yellowish green leaves unfold and grow.

The maple leaf forever

What leaf is pictured on the Canadian flag and penny? If you said the maple leaf, you're right. The maple is the national tree of Canada. At least one species of maple tree grows in every province. Check a field guide to find out which maples grow in your province.

Maple trees are important in their forest habitats. They provide food and homes to many different animals, including insects, birds, squirrels and raccoons. When the leaves fall and rot, they release nutrients that are used by other plants to grow.

Sugar Maples are used to make delicious maple syrup. Although maple trees grow all over the world, maple syrup is made only in Canada and the United States.

MAKE SOME MAPLE SYRUP

If you have a Sugar Maple or Black Maple in your yard, you can tap it to make maple syrup. The tree should be at least 75 cm around. The sap starts flowing in early spring when the daytime temperatures are above 0°C, but the nighttime temperatures are below freezing.

You'll need:

plastic or metal spiles (available from a hardware store)

a hand drill with an 11 mm drill bit

a hammer

2-L plastic pop bottles with lids

scissors

thin wire

a pail

a large pot

a stove

some felt

a funnel

containers with tight-fitting lids

a ladle

small sticks or dowelling, same size as spiles

1. Ask an adult to help you drill one hole on each side of the tree, about 1 m above the ground and 8 cm deep. Fit the spiles into the holes, and tap them gently with the hammer so they're firm.

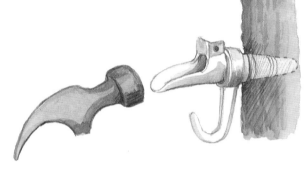

2. Cut a hole 4 cm from the bottom of each bottle. Turn each bottle upside down, tighten the lid and fit the hole snugly over a spile. Tie the bottles securely to the tree with wire.

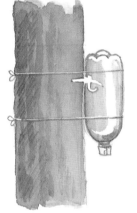

3. Twice a day put your pail under each pop bottle and remove its lid to collect the sap. Replace the lid tightly. Store your sap in the large pot in a cold area or a refrigerator until the pot is full.

4. Ask an adult to boil the sap for several hours. As the water evaporates, the sap becomes darker, thicker and sweeter. Eventually it turns into maple syrup. When the syrup tastes right, ask an adult to take it off the stove.

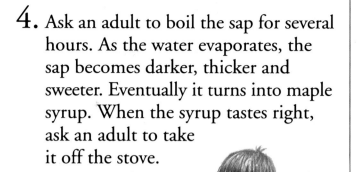

5. Put some damp felt in the top of the funnel to act as a filter. Rest the funnel in the top of a container and ladle syrup into the funnel. Put the lids on tightly. Store your syrup in a cool, dark place or a refrigerator or freezer.

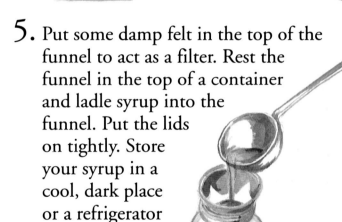

6. When the sap stops running in three weeks or so, take the spiles out of the trees and hammer small sticks or dowelling into the holes. The sticks will stop insects and fungi from getting into the tree and damaging it.

Canadian forests

If you were walking through a forest on the southwest coast of British Columbia, you would see different trees than someone hiking in a forest in Quebec. That's because each kind of tree needs its own special combination of soil and climate to grow well. Canada has eight different forest regions where certain tree species grow best. Look at the map to find out what forest regions are found in your province.

You can see on the map that not everyone in Canada lives in a forest region. People in southern Alberta, Saskatchewan and Manitoba may live in the dry prairie grasslands. People who live in the far north may live on the tundra, a wet, treeless area.

The place where the boreal forest stops growing and the tundra begins is called the tree line. Here the soils are too poor and the temperatures are too cold for trees to grow well. Another tree line is found in the mountains. The lower parts of the mountain slopes are often covered with trees, but higher up the soil is too thin and the winds are too strong and cold for trees to survive.

Forest Regions	Main Tree Species
■ **Boreal** (Mostly forest)	White Spruce, Black Spruce, Balsam Fir, Jack Pine, White Birch
■ **Boreal** (Forest and barren)	White Spruce, Black Spruce, Tamarack
■ **Boreal** (Forest and grass)	Trembling Aspen, willow
■ **Subalpine**	Engelmann Spruce, Alpine Fir, Lodgepole Pine
■ **Montane**	Douglas Fir, Lodgepole and Ponderosa Pine, Trembling Aspen
■ **Coast**	Western Red Cedar, Western Hemlock, Sitka Spruce
■ **Columbia**	Western Red Cedar, Western Hemlock, Douglas Fir
■ **Deciduous**	American Beech, Sugar Maple, Black Walnut
■ **Great Lakes-St. Lawrence**	Eastern White Pine, Red Pine, Eastern Hemlock, Yellow Birch
■ **Acadian**	Red Spruce, Balsam Fir, Yellow Birch, maple

Other Regions

■ **Grasslands**	
■ **Tundra**	

A Canadian rainforest

When you hear the word "rainforest" you may think of steamy, hot jungles, but did you know that Canada has its own kind of rainforest? The coast forest region of British Columbia has a temperate climate — it is very wet and mild — so plants can grow larger than anywhere else in Canada. In fact, all of the largest and oldest trees in Canada grow in British Columbia's temperate rainforest. Some trees are over 1000 years old and are as tall as a 30-storey building!

If you walked into the rainforest and looked up, you would see huge Western Hemlock, Sitka Spruce and Western Red Cedar. If you looked down, you would find the forest floor thickly covered with mosses, ferns and fungi. The rainforest is a wonderful habitat for wildlife, too, from the magnificent grizzly bear to the yellow-and-black banana slug.

Some of the rainforest habitat is protected in parks, but much of it is being destroyed by logging. Some environmentalists believe that almost all of British Columbia's unprotected rainforest will be gone in less than thirty years. New trees are being planted to replace the ones that are cut down, but it takes hundreds of years to form a rainforest habitat. Even if a new rainforest is allowed to grow, it will never be the same as the one that was destroyed. This is why many people across the country and around the world are asking Canadian governments to save more temperate rainforest before it's too late.

A temperate rainforest gets up to 4 metres of rain per year. That's enough to cover a one-storey house!

Big Red

The largest Red Cedar in the world grows on Vancouver Island, British Columbia. This tree probably started growing about 2000 years ago. It is as tall as a 20-storey building, and you would have to join hands with at least five friends to reach around its trunk!

Fruit trees

Juicy peaches, crisp apples and sweet plums are just some of the tasty treats that grow in orchards across the country. Canada has some of the best orchard-growing land in the world.

In the spring, pink and white blossoms fill the orchards with sweet perfume and attract thousands of honey bees. When the bees visit each flower to drink nectar and collect pollen for food, their hairy bodies become covered with pollen. When they visit the next flower, some of the pollen drops off and pollinates it. Once the flower has been pollinated, seeds begin to develop inside a thick, soft covering called a fruit. The fruit protects the seeds while they are developing, and it also attracts wildlife that eat the fruit and spread the seeds in their droppings.

Three of the best fruit-growing areas in Canada are the Okanagan Valley in British Columbia, the Niagara Fruit Belt in southern Ontario and the Annapolis Valley in Nova Scotia. The next time you go to the grocery store or local market, look to see how many of the fruits for sale were grown in Canada.

DRY SOME FRUIT SNACKS

You can dry some apples or pears in the fall and have delicious fruit snacks all winter long. Dried fruits make great snacks for hikes and camping trips, too.

You'll need:

some fresh apples and pears

an apple peeler

a knife

two cookie sheets

an oven

plastic bags

twist ties

1. Ask an adult to help you peel, core and thinly slice a few apples and pears.

2. Lay the fruit slices flat on the cookie sheets so that the slices do not overlap.

3. Have an adult preheat the oven to 100°C (200°F). Turn the oven off and place the cookie sheets in the oven for several hours. Reheat the oven every hour or so. When the fruit looks wrinkled, turn the slices over and dry them for a few more hours.

4. When the fruit looks and feels dry, put snack-size servings into small plastic bags and tie them tightly with twist ties. This keeps moisture from getting back into your fruit. Store the fruit in a cool, dry place.

If you have a fireplace or wood stove, you can dry some fruit the way your grandparents might have done it when they were kids. Thread your fruit slices on a string using a large darning needle. Ask an adult to hang the string of fruit from the mantle where the heat from the fire will dry the fruit quickly.

A terrific tree house

Trees make terrific homes for many animals, from tiny insects to Pine Martens and Great Blue Herons. All kinds of different animals may share one tree, using it for food, shelter and a place to raise their young. Birds often nest in tree holes or build their nests in the branches of trees. They feed on the tree's fruits and seeds, or on the insects that also live in the trees. Trees provide perches where birds can rest, as well as shelter from the cold and snow in winter. In this picture you'll see several tree-loving birds, as well as other animals that depend on trees for their survival. The next time you are out for a walk in the woods, see how many animals you can find at home in the trees.

Tree house trivia

Did you know . . .

. . . the Red-breasted Nuthatch smears a ring of sticky resin from pine trees around the entrance to its nesting cavity, possibly to keep out intruders?

. . . some ducks are born high up in trees? Wood Ducks, Buffleheads, Common Goldeneyes and Hooded and Common Mergansers all nest in tree cavities.

. . . Hairy Woodpeckers often carve out their nesting holes below a shelf of fungus growing on a tree trunk? The fungus works as an awning to shelter the nest.

Tree watching

Trees of all shapes and sizes grow throughout most of Canada. Tree watching is a great, year-round hobby no matter where you live. Choose a tree in your neighbourhood and watch it throughout the seasons. Deciduous trees show more changes during the year than conifers. Draw pictures or take photos of the tree when it flowers in spring, spreads its green leaves in summer, drops its colourful leaves in fall, and stands bare and cold in winter. Using the checklist on these pages and a good field guide to trees, you can learn to identify your tree and others that you see.

Tree watching checklist

Leaves

Are the leaves needlelike or scalelike?

Are the leaves broad and flat?

Are they simple or compound?

What shape are the leaves?

Are there teeth along the edges of the leaves?

Are the leaves hairy or smooth?

Are the leaves growing opposite each other on the twig or are they arranged alternately?

What colour are the leaves in the summer and the fall?

Flowers and fruit

Does the tree have flowers or cones?

If it has cones, what shape and size are they? Do they grow at the top of the tree or from the tips of the branches?

What colour, shape and size are the flowers?

When ripe, is the fruit hard like a nut or soft like a berry? What colour is it?

What shape, size and colour are the seeds?

Bark

Is the bark rough or smooth?

Is it scaly, stringy, flaky, peeling or ridged?

What colour is the bark?

Buds

Are the buds pointed or rounded?

Are they sticky or dry?

Do the buds smell?

How are the buds arranged on the twig, opposite or alternate?

Silhouettes

What is the general shape of the tree?

Is it wider at the top or the bottom?

Is it pointed or rounded at the top?

Does it have branches all the way down its trunk or only part way down?

Trees and you

Look around your home and try to count all of the things that are made from trees. Include food, wood and paper products. Now imagine your home without any tree products. Trees and their products are part of our lives every day.

Trees are even more important in nature. They provide homes and food for wildlife. Their leaves and branches supply cooling shade and shelter from harsh winds. Tree roots hold onto the soil to keep it from being washed away. And during photosynthesis, trees take in carbon dioxide from the air and give off oxygen that wildlife and people need to breathe.

Tree talk

Trees don't have to talk to tell you about themselves. You can discover how old a tree was when it was cut down, or how much it grew in the last few seasons, just by looking at it closely.

If you find an old tree stump in the woods, examine the cut end. Wet the wood a bit and you'll see a pattern of light and dark rings. The light rings show the fast spring and early summer growth of the tree. The dark rings show the slower growth of late summer and early fall. Each pair of light and dark rings counts for one year of growth. Starting at the centre of the stump, count the pairs of rings. This will tell you how old the tree was when it was cut.

spring and early summer growth

bark

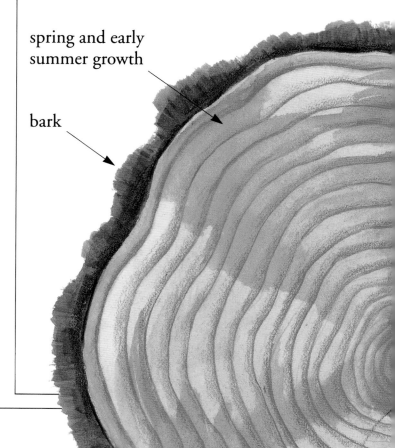

Winter is a great time to look at the twigs of deciduous trees, since they are bare and easy to see. Find a bumpy ring around a twig, close to the tip. This marks the beginning of last year's growth. The distance from this ring to the tip of the twig tells you how much the twig grew last spring and summer. You can keep track of how well the trees in your yard or neighbourhood are growing by checking their twigs each winter. Which kind of tree is the fastest grower in your area? Which is the slowest?

late summer and early fall growth

Canada's provincial trees

As well as Canada's national symbol, the maple tree, many provinces have chosen their own provincial tree. What is your provincial tree? The Yukon has not named a provincial tree yet.

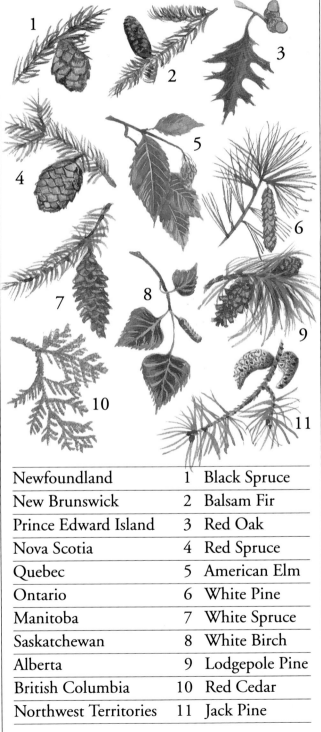

Newfoundland	1	Black Spruce
New Brunswick	2	Balsam Fir
Prince Edward Island	3	Red Oak
Nova Scotia	4	Red Spruce
Quebec	5	American Elm
Ontario	6	White Pine
Manitoba	7	White Spruce
Saskatchewan	8	White Birch
Alberta	9	Lodgepole Pine
British Columbia	10	Red Cedar
Northwest Territories	11	Jack Pine

Endangered trees

If an animal is in danger, it can sometimes run away or hide to keep safe. Trees can't protect themselves when they are attacked by insects or disease, cut down, or when their habitat is destroyed. Some trees in Canada are listed as endangered or threatened and may die out completely unless something is done to protect them.

All of the trees listed as endangered and threatened in Canada grow in the deciduous forest zone in southwestern Ontario.

Destruction of their habitat for logging, farming and construction of roads and houses is causing these trees to die. Fortunately, some trees are protected in parks and nature reserves. Conservation groups and local governments are also teaching local landowners about the need to protect the habitats of these species.

YOU CAN HELP

You can help to protect the trees in your neighbourhood and across Canada by telling your friends and family how important trees are in nature and in our lives. Read on to discover some ways to help trees.

1. Remind your friends never to pull bark off trees or to carve in it. The bark protects the tree from insects, fungi and disease that can hurt or kill the tree.

2. Ask your parents not to cut down trees on your property. Plant new trees if you have the space. Trees provide food and shelter for birds and other wildlife.

3. Write to your local town or city council and ask them to plant more trees along the streets or in the parks. Explain why trees are important.

4. Ask your teacher if your class can plant a tree at school and care for it. This is a good Arbour Day or Earth Day event.

5. Raise money for a conservation group that is working to protect trees in Canada. Have a sale of reusable tree products such as books, magazines and items made of wood.

6. Help to save trees by reducing, reusing and recycling tree products. Ask your parents to buy recycled paper products. Avoid using disposable plates, napkins and cups. Choose products with little or no packaging. Recycle newspapers, writing and computer paper and cardboard. Always write on both sides of paper.

Did you know that for every tonne of recycled paper that is made, 17 trees are saved?

Grow a tree

You can grow a tree in your backyard or on a balcony by planting seeds. Why not plant a tree on your birthday or for someone else's special day to celebrate the event? Your gift may last a lifetime. Choose a place where the tree will have room to grow and won't be in the way of other activities in the yard. You can collect seeds from nearby trees or from locally grown fruit, or buy them at a garden centre. Once your tree is planted, take care of it to make sure it survives. Watch how your tree grows and changes throughout the seasons and keep notes about the wildlife that visit it.

You'll need:

seeds from trees such as apple, horse chestnut, maple, peach or walnut

a shovel

compost (optional)

water

gravel and potting soil

a large, plastic flowerpot (optional)

1. If you are using local seeds, collect and plant them in the fall, or look for sprouted seeds on the ground in the spring. A sprouted seed is cracked with a tiny, white root coming out. It may also have two small, green leaves growing out of it. Check the ground for sprouted seeds near maples, horse chestnuts, elms, oaks and other trees that produce lots of seeds.

2. Dig a small hole in the ground where you want your tree to grow. Loosen the soil inside the hole to help the tree roots spread more easily. Put some compost in the hole and water it.

3. Gently place the seed in the hole and cover it with soil. If the seed has already sprouted, be careful not to break off the tiny root. Keep the green leaves above the soil.

4. A small garden fence or some branches laid around your seedling will help to keep people and pets from stepping on it.

5. If you are planting your seed in a pot, put gravel in the bottom of the pot for drainage before filling the pot with soil. Dig a small hole and fill it with water. Plant your seed in it and cover it with soil. Native trees should be left outside all winter.

6. As your tree grows bigger, it may need a tall wooden stake beside it to provide support for the trunk.

Index

A
age of a tree, 26

B
bark, 4, 13, 29
birds, 22–23
buds, 13

C
Canada's national tree, 14, 27
chlorophyll, 8, 10–11
compound leaves, 8
cones, 6–7
coniferous trees, 6–7, 24
conservation, 18, 28–29

D
deciduous trees, 6–7, 24, 28

E
endangered trees, 18, 28–29

F
features of a tree, 4–5, 24–25
flowers, 6, 20
forest fires, 7
forest regions of Canada,
        16–17, 28
fruit, 6, 20, 22
    drying, 21
fruit trees, 20–21

G
growing a tree, 30–31
growth of a tree, 18, 19
    measuring, 27

L
leaf collecting, 9
leaves, 5, 8–9, 14, 26
    colours of, 8, 10–11
    falling off, 6, 12
    inside a bud, 13
    shapes of, 8

M
maple syrup, 14–15
maple trees, 6, 14, 27

N
needles, 6

O
orchards, 20

P
people and trees, 4, 14, 20, 26
    See also endangered trees
photosynthesis, 8, 26
planting a tree, 30–31
pollination, 6, 20
provincial trees, 27

R
rainforests, 18–19
roots, 4, 26

S
seeds, 5, 6–7, 20, 22, 30–31
simple leaves, 8
species in Canada, 4, 14,
        16–17

T
trees in nature, 4, 14, 22–23,
        26
    See also wildlife and trees
tree line, 16–17
tree parts, 4–5, 24–25
tree products, 4, 14, 20, 26,
        29
tree rings, 26
tree watching, 24–25, 26–27,
        30

W
wildlife and trees, 4, 14, 18,
        20, 22–23, 26
winter, 12–13, 22, 27